The Red Arrows
Story

Also in this series:

1. *The Concorde Story*, first published 2005
2. *The Spitfire Story*, first published 2006
3. *The Vulcan Story*, first published 2006

The Red Arrows Story

Peter R. March

Sutton Publishing

Sutton Publishing Limited
Phoenix Mill, Thrupp, Stroud
Gloucestershire, GL5 2BU

First published 2006

British Library Cataloguing in Publication Data
A catalogue for this book is available from the British Library.

ISBN 0-7509-4446-3

Typeset in 9.5/14.5pt Syntax.
Typesetting and origination by
Sutton Publishing Limited.
Printed and bound in England by
J.H. Haynes & Co. Ltd, Sparkford.

➤
(Jamie Hunter)

The story of the Royal Air Force Aerobatic Team, the Red Arrows, is not difficult to tell. A great deal has been written in books, magazines, newspapers and brochures in the years since the team was formed as part of the Central Flying School in 1965. What is more demanding is to find new information concerning both past and recent activities. I am therefore very grateful to Glen Moreman for giving me an account of the team's 'Kemble Years' and some interesting contemporary photographs to use in this book.

Jamie Hunter's description of a flight with the Red Arrows in April 2006, the introductory account of the team's Springhawk pre-season training at RAF Akrotiri, Cyprus, and an outstanding collection of air-to-air photographs has given new life to the story. I am also grateful to Mike Jorgensen/Air Action Images for allowing me to use some of his recent photos of the team in Cyprus.

Selecting a relatively small number from the huge stock of Red Arrows' Hawk photographs available to me was a nice problem to have. I would like to thank Gordon Bartley, Katsuhiko Tokunaga, Adrian Balch, Pete Mobbs and Daniel March for providing so many outstanding images that capture both the routine and the significant moments in the Red Arrows' years.

Once again I am indebted to Brian Strickland for his patient research, both for the text and the photographs. I have also received help from Ben Dunnell and Michael J.F. Bowyer, and through the published works of former Red Arrows manager Andy Stewart and public relations officer Tony Cunnane.

I would like to dedicate this small book to the memory of the late Ray Hanna. There is no doubt that his skilled leadership from 1966 to 1969 set the team on its incredible path to worldwide acclaim. Ray epitomised the excellence of the Red Arrows throughout forty years of airshow flying, initially while serving with the RAF and subsequently while displaying his Spitfire IX, MH434, and other warbirds.

Photo Credits

Photographs Peter R. March/PRM Aviation Collection unless otherwise credited.

'I was closely connected with the Red Arrows when we were flying from Fairford, and they were at Kemble, a short distance away, in the early 1970s. In fact I was in pre-production Concorde 01 when it flew in formation with the Red Arrows, and vividly remember that occasion. In those days the team flew the Gnat.

I was privileged to have a flight in the leader's Gnat for a formation practice. I was fascinated by it. I expected the whole thing would be too much for me, but I was impressed by the smoothness with which everything was done. This was all down to the leader's skill and the ability of the other team members to follow accordingly. These pilots are very highly trained and very talented, but above all they are an immense national asset.

They bring great credit on this country, and we should remember that when we hear talk of defence cuts and wonder if the Red Arrows is going to fall victim. That should never happen. The team is a great national institution, and I wish them many more years of flying.'

The late Brian Trubshaw, chief test pilot of Concorde

➤➤

Red Arrows Hawks pass in 'Concorde' formation.

◄◄

Brian Trubshaw flying the pre-production Concorde G-AXDN, led by the Red Arrows' scarlet-painted Gnats. (Arthur Gibson Collection)

Did you know?

The swept-wing Folland Gnat was designed as a lightweight fighter, and was described by the Red Arrows as the 'pocket rocket'.

The Royal Air Force's Red Arrows, recognised the world over as one of the top military jet aerobatic display teams, has been displaying for over forty years and has given some 4,000 public performances.

The team is one of Britain's great international ambassadors and the showpiece of the Royal Air Force (RAF), demonstrating the skills and airmanship in a tradition that goes back to the 1920s. It is universally acknowledged wherever it performs, both for its brilliant displays and the qualities of the aircraft it flies, the BAe Hawk advanced jet trainer. Very much the public face of the RAF, the team enhances the Service's reputation on many fronts and has been of considerable benefit to British trade and industry. BAE Systems, which manufacturers the latest version of the Hawk, has been able to build on the team's high profile on overseas visits,

to encourage an interest in the aircraft by air arms in many countries. This has helped to secure multi-million-pound contracts for the company, for engine manufacturer Rolls-Royce, and for a host of other aviation companies around the UK.

'The Red Arrows stand alone. They are appreciated and have achieved the basic essential in aerobatic demonstration, which is unbroken continuity of manoeuvre from take-off to landing.'

Gp Capt Sir Douglas Bader

Up to the end of 2005 the Red Arrows had given 3,928 displays in 50 different countries, from Australia and Zimbabwe to Bangladesh and the Ukraine. The appreciative crowds have ranged from just a few hundred at Goose Bay to a staggering 650,000 in Portugal in June 1973 and nearly a million along the Sydney waterfront in 1996.

The team's nine-aircraft, close-formation routines and breathtaking sequences by the 'synchro' performers have been the subject of many hours of colourful television programmes beamed across the world and watched by countless viewers.

Established in 1965, the team was initially based at RAF Fairford, Gloucestershire, which was then a satellite of the RAF's Central Flying School (CFS). It comprised seven display pilots flying red-painted Folland/Hawker Siddeley Gnat advanced training aircraft.

In its first full year the Red Arrows team gave sixty-five displays in Britain, France, Italy, Holland, Belgium and Germany. In 1968 the team was extended to fly nine Gnats. Since then the signature 'diamond nine' formation has come to represent the peak of precision flying, and is now the team's trademark that is recognised worldwide.

The team took delivery of Hawk T.1 jet trainers in late 1979, the pilots converting from Gnats and working up using the new aircraft in time for the 1980 summer display season.

The Red Arrows team remains today a standard RAF squadron with the primary role in peacetime of demonstrating the teamwork and excellence of performance demanded of all RAF personnel.

◄
Hawks replaced the Gnats in 1979 and still equip the team today.

◄◄
The Red Arrows first flew bright-red-painted Gnats from 1965 to 1979.

Did you know?
The highest number of displays flown by the Reds in any one calendar year was 136 in 1995. The total included the autumn tour of Africa, Middle East and Far East.

It is becoming hard to recall a time when the Red Arrows was not the RAF's premier display team. In fact you have to go back to 1964, and to the Red Pelicans of the CFS to find the Arrows' predecessor. The last RAF aerobatic team to fly front-line fighters was 56 Squadron's Firebirds team with nine red-and-silver English Electric Lightnings in 1963.

Without doubt the most famous operational aircraft to be flown by the RAF's premier team was the Hawker Hunter. In 1957 five black-painted Hunters of 111 Squadron, which became known as the Black Arrows, was formed. At Farnborough the following year 'Treble One' Squadron provided the spectacle of a twenty-two-Hunter loop, the greatest number of aircraft ever looped in formation. The Black Arrows continued as the RAF's aerobatic team until

◄

Lightnings of 56 Squadron displaying at Farnborough in 1963.

◄◄

Representing teams past and present. A Yellowjacks' painted Gnat and Black Arrows and Blue Diamonds Hunters join the Red Arrows for a fly-past at Biggin Hill, September 2005.

1961, when it was replaced by the Blue Diamonds of 92 Squadron.

The Lightnings of 74 Squadron, The Tigers, were given the leading role in 1962, and 56 Squadron, The Firebirds, took the mantle in 1963. It was decided in that year, for operational and economic reasons, that the RAF's leading team should be drawn from a training unit rather than from front-line fighter squadrons. So in 1964 the Red Pelicans, flying six Jet Provost T.4s, became the first CFS team to be given the leading role for over thirty years. Despite an extremely polished aerobatic display, the relatively slow and ungainly Jet Provost compared unfavourably with the sleek Hunter and powerful Lightning, reducing the impact of the team's performance.

'Aerobatic and formation flying is a military necessity for fighter pilots. Combine the two, add some coloured smoke, and the result is terrific. I could use more superlatives in praising the Red Arrows, but let me finish by quoting the highest praise they will ever receive. Last year [1968] the announcer at an international air show said as the Gnats started their display: "Here come the Red Arrows, the best aerobatic team in the world" – and that is a very handsome tribute when you realise it was a French announcer speaking at a French Air Show.'

Gp Capt Sir Douglas Bader

In 1964 an aerobatic team was formed at No. 4 Flying Training School (FTS) at RAF Valley in Wales to see if the Gnat T.1 could effectively be used as an economic display aircraft. It was formed of yellow-painted Gnats flown by Instructors led by Flt Lt Lee Jones, with the title Yellowjacks. While Lee Jones was well qualified to lead the Gnat team, having previously been a member of the Black Arrows, the famous Hunter team that had represented the RAF at Farnborough in 1964 alongside the Red Pelicans, there was

The Yellowjacks prepare to taxi at CFS Little Rissington in August 1964.

Did you know?

It was decided when the Yellowjacks were flying that the colour yellow was difficult to follow, and the public often lost the aircraft on poor-visibility days. Red was found to be much better, enabling the aircraft to be seen throughout most of the formation flying. When the team changed from the Gnat to the Hawk it also changed from Post Office red on the Gnat to signal red on the Hawk. The red, white and blue fin flash of the Gnat was retained on the Hawk, and the white lightning flash down the side was extended to meet the white of the tail marking on the Hawk.

some uncertainty about the aircraft. The Gnat had only entered service in 1962 and still had a number of teething problems. The Aeroplane and Armament Experimental Establishment at Boscombe Down had warned, in a handling assessment, that it might not prove very practicable for formation aerobatics.

However, the team found it could put on a good show and was able to overcome the initial unimpressive nature of the Gnat, which lacked the fantastic noise and visible fires of the supersonic types on full reheat. This was achieved by sheer grace, precision and an extended repertoire of formation changes.

The Yellowjacks team was allocated ten aircraft (XR540, XR901–6, XR986–7 and XS111) for its five-ship display routine. As it transpired this was an unnecessarily generous provision.

The Gnat was an ideal compromise between the front-line jet fighter and the less-attractive jet trainers. The aircraft's classic swept wing lent itself to symmetrical formation shapes and hitherto unsurpassed manoeuvres. This was accompanied by an accuracy of control that assured slick and precise formation changes. It brought back the sleek appearance to which the public had grown accustomed in the formation displays of earlier years.

◄◄

Yellow-painted Gnats of the aptly named Yellowjacks team performed at Farnborough in September 1964.
(via Adrian Balch)

The Yellowjacks team gave its first public display at the Royal Naval Air Station (RNAS) Culdrose Air Day on 25 July 1964 and proved an instant success. This was underlined by the reception it received after appearing at the Farnborough Air Show in September, which influenced the decision to establish the new Gnat team as part of the CFS, which at that time was based at RAF Little Rissington in Gloucestershire. The team was to be run on the lines of a normal RAF squadron, but dedicated wholly to aerobatic flying at air displays and on other occasions. However, one major problem had to be overcome. The

Did you know?

There were only seven display pilots in 1965, 1966 and 1971.

team had been named the Yellowjacks because of the yellow-painted Gnats it flew. But the then commandant of the CFS, Air Cdre Bird-Wilson, apparently hated the title and insisted on a name change.

Lee Jones, who had no fear of senior officers, appeared to acquiesce to authority, and for a short time the team was known by the preposterous name Daffodils. The Gnats were then painted red, probably to ensure that the name Yellowjacks (or Daffodils) could no longer be used. When asked by Bird-Wilson to suggest a name for the new team, he said: 'Let it be Red Arrows – Red for the colour, and Arrows in memory of the Black Arrows'.

Like the Red Pelicans before it, the new team was established on an annual basis as part of the CFS. It was officially dubbed the Red Arrows, adopting the colour associated with the CFS and the arrow-like shape of the Gnat and its formations from the earlier Treble One Squadron Hunter team. The ten red-painted Gnats were initially based at RAF Fairford as a CFS detachment.

The Red Arrows' public debut in the UK was at the Biggin Hill Air Fair in May 1965, and it was followed by over sixty appearances, including visits to Belgium, France, Italy, the Netherlands and West Germany. At the end of 1965 the team was awarded the Britannia Trophy by the Royal Aero Club in recognition of its outstanding contribution to British prestige in the field of aviation.

The year 1966 saw the advent of the seven-aircraft team under the leadership of newly promoted Sqn Ldr Ray Hanna, and just

Did you know?
The first public display in the UK was at the International Air Fair at Biggin Hill on 16 May 1965.

◄
Yellowjacks Gnats flying with the 1964 RAF Aerobatic Team, the Red Pelicans.

under ninety shows had been flown by the end of the season. Technical problems with the Gnat, which required a detailed structural check of each aircraft, delayed the start of the 1967 season, but nevertheless nearly 100 public appearances were made during the season. If offered a choice between a Spitfire and a Gnat, former Red Arrows leader the late Ray Hanna would give the unequivocal response: 'Both, please!'

In 1968 a team of nine pilots, without reserves, was approved. Since then the Red Arrows' 'diamond nine' formation has come to represent the peak of formation flying. Such was the team's outstanding success that in 1969, Ray Hanna's final year as leader, it was decided to establish the Red Arrows permanently within the CFS, with the equivalent status of a full RAF squadron.

◄
Seven Gnats of the RAF Aerobatic Team in action.

Did you know?
Nine Gnat displays were given in Italy and Germany before the British public were able to watch the big formation display at Brawdy on 6 August 1966.

Did you know?
The first Red Arrows display for the public was in France, at the French National Air Day at Clermont Ferrand on 9 May 1965.

➤
The 1966 team, with Sqn Ldr Ray Hanna at its forefront. With him are Flt Lt Derek Bell (Red 2), Flt Lt Bill Langworthy (Red 3), Flt Lt Peter Evans (Red 4), Flt Lt Roy Booth (Red 5), Flt Lt Henry Prince (Red 6), Flt Lt Timothy Nelson (Red 7), Flt Lt Frank Hoare (Red 8) and Flt Lt Douglas McGregor (Red 9).

Biggin Hill Air Fair organiser Jock Maitland greets Ray Hanna on his arrival at the 1967 event. Note that the aircraft is in regular training livery. The leader had to borrow a 'standard' Gnat that day after structural checks grounded his usual red-painted aircraft.

13

➤
Very occasionally the team displayed still carrying underwing fuel tanks, as here at Halfpenny Green in September 1969.

➤➤
The long-range fuel tanks that could be carried after 1966 changed the Gnat's profile appreciably.

Although the CFS was officially based at RAF Little Rissington, because of the Gnat's higher speed and the rather crowded airfield circuit, the Red Arrows' ten aircraft, plus a further twelve Gnats of 'C' Flight of the CFS, were detached to RAF Fairford in 1965. The following year they moved across to self-contained accommodation on 'G' site at RAF Kemble, just 10 miles to the west and still in Gloucestershire. The team took advantage of the quieter circuit, and used the end of Runway 13 as a parking area for

14

the Gnats and any other visiting aircraft during the summer months.

In October 1966 the Red Arrows' Gnats were cleared by the test pilots at Boscombe Down to use 'slipper' fuel tanks under the wings, enabling them to travel much greater distances. Until then their range had been severely limited because two of the integral fuselage tanks were adapted for storing the diesel oil that, when injected into the exhaust, created the smoke.

Early 1967 saw the construction of a new aircraft servicing pan opposite 'G' site specifically for the CFS detachment, and it was

Did you know?

The Gnat went overseas in Europe, but not very far afield, though underwing fuel tanks were used to reach the furthest points, such as Scandinavia, Finland and Malta.

➤➤
A sick pilot meant an eight-ship display, and produced some unusual Gnat formations.

officially handed over in April. Shortly afterwards the Reds began returning from Little Rissington following their winter servicing programme, bearing the first signs of the relaxation of an Air Ministry ban on over-zealous paint schemes. Through Ray Hanna's persistence the fins were painted red, white and blue, but the team had to wait another year before it was able to apply a white lightning stripe along the side of the fuselage.

The Gnat was an extremely agile and quiet aircraft, and these were qualities that all of its pilots enjoyed, especially the Reds. They allowed the pilots to sneak over the Tetbury road across the airfield at very low level, beating-up the flight line or the runway controller's caravan. Any unsuspecting members of the groundcrew were then doused in the diesel fumes from the smoke and smelt of them for the rest of the day. For a dare, a couple of Red Arrows pilots took up a challenge to see who could fly the lowest through the 'V' shape formed by the roofs of the two 'G' site hangars, the winner being the one who deposited the most coloured dye on the surfaces.

A very special bond between the Arrows (as the team was always locally known) and Kemble village remains to this day. Long after they left, the team, if it was transiting the area, would regularly treat the villagers to a fly-past with red, white and blue smoke in recognition of that support.

Through the 1970s the team had a succession of six leaders, with eight further pilots and a manager, the latter flying the 'spare' aircraft to displays and 'performing' as commentator. In 1973 the Arrows gave 103 public displays during the season,

19

topping the 100 mark for the first time. The fuel crisis of 1974 prevented the team from giving public displays until July that year. In the first 10 years over 800 displays were given, and the 1,000th performance came in 1977 at the International Air Tattoo at RAF Greenham Common. By the end of the 1979 season, when the Gnats were

➤

Ray Hanna at very low level at Kemble.
(via Glen Moreman)

➤➤

The Red Arrows, here reduced to seven aircraft because of the fuel crisis, displaying at RAF Chivenor in 1974.

scheduled to be replaced by the new BAe Hawk T.1, the team had given 1,292 public performances, entailing visits to eighteen overseas countries.

The Red Arrows took delivery of the Hawk in the winter of 1979/80, and undertook the task of converting the pilots from Gnat to Hawk. It introduced two new team

◄

Hawks replaced Gnats by November 1979, and the Red Arrows flew the new aircraft the following season.
(Daniel J. March)

◄◄

The team lined up at a very wet RAF Turnhouse, Edinburgh, in June 1971.

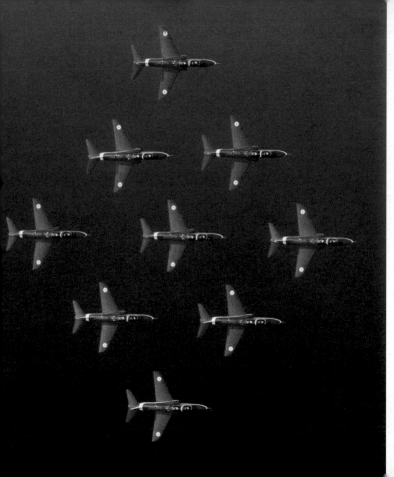

members and worked up a display using a completely new aeroplane in time for the start of the 1980 season.

The Red Arrows left Kemble for the last time on 10 March 1983, when the team headed out to RAF Akrotiri in Cyprus for its annual work-up to the forthcoming display season. Two days earlier it had performed a ceremonial fly-past over Cirencester and given a final display over the airfield. On returning to the UK the team went straight to its new home at RAF Scampton, Lincolnshire.

'No Red Arrows display would be complete, nor would be so effective, without smoke.'
Michael Bonello

◄

After returning to England and occupying its new base at RAF Scampton in April 1983, the team soon settled into a busy season of displays.

◄◄

After departing Kemble for Cyprus in March 1983, the Reds did not return to the Cotswolds base.
(BAe Defence)

27

➤

A dramatic view of the Red Arrows looping over Victoria Falls during the visit to southern Africa in 1995.

(Air Cdre Simon Bostock)

As the more versatile Hawk had a greater range, the team was able to travel more widely, not only in Britain and Europe, but also on major tours to North America, the Middle East and Scandinavia. The first tour to the Far East was completed in 1986. It entailed giving twenty-two displays in fifteen countries, and travelling 18,500 miles in six weeks. Primarily the team performs the function of representing the RAF at individual aviation events around the world, but it is increasingly promoting 'British excellence', and especially the very successful Hawk, which remains in production by BAE Systems today.

Since 1965 the team has performed worldwide, flown nearly 4,000 displays and visited the following countries. The figures in brackets are the total number of displays given in the respective countries. Bangladesh (1),

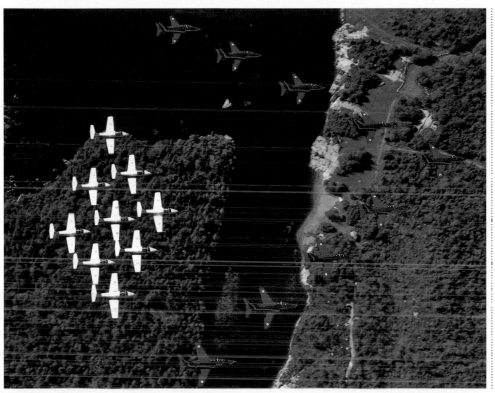

During a short visit to Canada in the autumn of 2002 the Red Arrows made a formation fly-past over Niagara Falls with the Canadian Snowbirds team.
(E.J. Kongingsveld via RAFCTE)

Did you know?
Within hours of a Red Arrows display in Amman, Jordan, in 1966, a British businessman received an order from a Jordanian company for a million Christmas cards featuring the Red Arrows.

29

Did you know?

On one of their worldwide visits the team was transiting from Malawi to South Africa and was anticipating that the South African Air Force (SAAF) would intercept it at the border. The team had obtained air traffic control clearance for a cruise climb, and by the time it reached the border it was at 47,000ft. The SAAF's Cheetah fighters were unable to reach this height, so the Reds obligingly descended to be intercepted.

➤
A deployment to the Far East in July 1986, named Eastern Hawk, involved twenty-two displays in fifteen countries. The team is here seen transiting Saudi Arabia with two support Hercules.
(BAe Military Aircraft)

➤

A spectacular view of the Red Arrows displaying at Dubai while en route to South Africa.
(Peter Mobbs)

➤➤

The team visited North America in 1983 and 1993, and on both occasions flew over the Jefferson Memorial in Washington, DC.
(BAe Military Aircraft)

◄
Team leader Sqn Ldr Adrian Thurley signs autographs on the Houston crowdline.

◄◄
During the US tour in 1993 the Red Arrows gave an unexpected display at Houston, Texas, replacing the USAF Thunderbirds team at the last minute.

➤
There is no mistaking where the team is flying in this photograph. During Eastern Hawk 03 it visited ten countries, including Egypt.
(BAe Military Aircraft)

Hungary (1), India (1), Libya (1), Morocco (1), Philippines (1), Poland (1), Slovakia (1); Bahrain (2), Czech Republic (2), Eire (2), Greece (2), Iceland (2), Luxembourg (2), Monaco (2), Oman (2), Portugal (2), Qatar (2), Ukraine (2), Zimbabwe (2); Australia (3), Brunei (3), Pakistan (3), Saudi Arabia (3), Thailand (3); Egypt (4), Turkey (4); Austria (5) Spain (5); Gibraltar (6); South Africa (7); Jordan (8), Singapore (8); Norway (9); Finland (10), Netherlands (10); Indonesia (12), Sweden (12); Canada (13); Malta (15); United Arab Emirates (UAE) (17); Denmark (18); Switzerland (20); Malaysia (24); Italy (32); USA (35); France (50); Cyprus (53); Belgium (75) and Germany (170).

Did you know?

The Red Arrows' tours to distant countries are generally part-funded by the UK aero industry, rather than the British taxpayer.

'We managed to do a show at Houston, Texas, at very short notice. The United States Air Force's Thunderbirds had to cancel, and were in New Orleans for a US tour. It was surprising to arrive at a show on a Sunday morning and to find 150,000 people at the airfield waiting to see us perform. In addition there was already a solid six-mile tailback on the adjoining Interstate highway of others waiting to get in to the show.'

Gp Capt Les Garside Beattie

One of the more difficult European display venues is Switzerland. Here the team is seen at Sion, where high mountains surround the airfield on all sides.

ROYAL AIR FORCE

Did you know?

The Red Arrows' Hawks are capable of carrying weapons for a wartime role. Some aircraft can carry a gun pod on the fuselage centreline and tanks on the wing. Others can augment the gun pod with AIM9I Sidewinder air-to-air missiles under the wings.

All Red Arrows pilots are volunteers. There are usually ten times more applications each year than places available. A paper pre-selection reduces this to a shortlist of around nine. To be eligible for the team, pilots are required to have completed at least one operational tour on a front-line fast jet (such as the Tornado, Harrier or Jaguar), and to have amassed at least 1,500 flying hours. Current annual reports must have ranked them as 'above average' in their flying role. Such provisos mean that the volunteers are usually flight lieutenants in their late 20s or early 30s.

The nine pilots selected for consideration are then attached to the Red Arrows for a short period. They meet the current team, fly in the back seats of the Hawks during display practice, and then undergo interviews. At that stage the shortlisted pilots are deemed to be capable of meeting the high standard of professional flying that is required. They have also been assessed on their personal qualities, together with their motivation. It is crucial that the nine display pilots in the team not only trust each other's skills, but also get on well together.

The current pilots then make the final choice at a 'closed' meeting (no outsiders are ever permitted) chaired by the Commandant of the CFS. Unsuccessful candidates can reapply, provided they still meet the selection criteria. The whole process is, therefore, very democratic, there being no other selection procedure like it in the RAF.

Usually each display pilot stays with the team for a three-year tour of duty. By changing three pilots each year the experience level within the team is optimised, there being three first-year pilots, three second-year pilots and three in their final year. The three new members usually join in September, to enable them to fly in the back seats with the team during the remaining displays of the season.

If a pilot goes sick during the display season, or for any other reason is unable to participate, the team can fly an eight-ship formation. For safety reasons there is never a reserve pilot. Team members always fly in the same position within the formation during that season.

When their tour is completed the pilots return to front-line squadrons to resume their mainstream career. A few leave the RAF at this stage to take up civilian flying positions.

The team leader, of squadron leader rank, will always have completed a three-year tour as a Red Arrows team pilot earlier in his career.

◀
Red 1 for the 2005–6 seasons, Sqn Ldr Dicky Patounas, had previously flown as a team member in 1998–2000.
(Jamie Hunter)

Did you know?
A week's in-season leave in August was introduced in 1972. This is seen as an essential break, and display organisers try to plan around it.

The Red Arrows team manager, known as 'Red 10', is responsible for the smooth running of the team and for ensuring that the flying demonstration is well organised. In addition he takes some of the workload from the team leader, the other team pilots and, to a lesser extent, assists with the engineering tasks.

The overall planning of the display season is his primary task. Over the years many displays have been flown in support of the RAF Careers Information Service, and this duty may include the targeting of specific schools and areas. Like any major industry, the RAF aims to recruit 'the best'. Consequently the team helps to encourage recruiting wherever it goes.

Detailed planning for the first display begins about six weeks before the event, when logistics requirements are sent to the display organiser. The team manager maintains close contact with the organisers over

'I remember coming back after a display at Mildenhall where we were to be parked just yards from the public. Opening the canopy, I heard this fantastic applause and you felt like looking around to see why they were clapping. It's very strange, for much of the time we are isolated from the airshow crowds.'

Flt Lt Jerry Bird, team member 1992–4

the following weeks. Two weeks before each display a military operation order is issued showing timings, transit routes, personnel involved and any equipment required.

The ten Hawks are usually flown to each operating airfield, the spare aircraft being flown by the manager, Red 10. The engineer officer and nine ground-crew members fly in the rear seats of the aircraft during transit flights so that servicing can begin immediately on arrival.

Before the display the pilots are briefed by the leader, who has to decide which sequences to fly according to the prevailing weather conditions. The manager normally gives the display commentary at each event.

Did you know?

The Red Arrows has a tenth Hawk pilot. Red 10 flies the reserve aircraft and often joins the team for its arrival and landing at a display airfield. He is the ground safety officer and team commentator.

'We were just completing a left-hand turn towards Scampton airfield, preparatory to running in for a flat break, when Red 2, immediately to my left, eased upwards out of the formation. I stayed with Ian [Smith] – that's the standard procedure. Almost immediately I could see that the whole of the top part of his canopy had disappeared.'

Sqn Ldr Andy Offer on 21 January 1998, while flying at 350mph, 400ft above open farmland north-west of Scampton, towards the end of a routine practice by six aircraft. Ian's aircraft had flown through a flock of lapwings, but he managed to land safely

➤

The Red Arrows' team manager flies the spare aircraft to some airshows. Here Red 10 is in the 'box' for the arrival at an airshow venue.

➤
One of the First-Line Blues marshals the leader to his parking slot at an airshow.

Did you know?

It is occasionally necessary for the aircraft to be swapped between team positions.

This can cause a problem, as the leader only uses white smoke, but some other team members, particularly the synchro pair, need all three colours.

The travelling ground crew, usually referred to as the Blues because of their blue suits and known as the 'First Line', are a close-knit team of eighty-five dedicated and skilled tradesmen. Each one is responsible for specific engineering tasks. They keep the Red Arrows' show on the road by providing the wide range of support necessary to ensure the smooth running of the team.

'For me, the most enjoyable aspect of being a member of the Red Arrows was undoubtedly the flying. There were no really low points to the job, although one has to say that the RAF hierarchy didn't always understand what we were trying to achieve, and they occasionally made life a little difficult.'
Gp Capt Brian Hoskins, during his time as a squadron leader with the Red Arrows

Keeping the Red Arrows in the air is a complex, time-consuming process. The working conditions are often difficult, tasks having to be carried out quickly in order to prepare the Hawks for the next flight, and allowing the performance of up to three displays in an afternoon.

Overall responsibility for the management of the Blues falls to the Senior and Junior Engineering Officers. The Senior Engineering Officer's ('Sengo') role is the long-term management of the team's fleet of eleven aircraft. The Junior Engineering Officer ('Jengo') ensures that Red 1 has sufficient aircraft to meet the daily task, whether that be training in winter or during the display season. Both officers are commissioned engineering officers selected for a two-year tour with the team, after which they leave for other engineering posts within the RAF.

◄

One important task for the ground crew is to clean the windscreens and canopies between flights.

47

The Blues move forward as the Hawks prepare to taxi for departure after displaying in Belgium.

ROYAL AIR FORCE

Nine of the tradesmen and the Engineering Officer are in the 'circus', which means they each fly as rear-seat passengers in the Hawk on transit flights. These are selected each December to form the select team for the following year. Each 'circus' member works with the same pilot throughout the season, and is responsible for the aircraft's flight servicing, as well as preparation of the pilot's flying kit.

Equally as important as the 'circus' are the remainder of the First Line, who travel by road (or by support Lockheed C-130K Hercules on overseas deployments). They provide the specialist support needed to rectify any minor faults that occur en route or during the display; and at these times they really come into their own.

During the winter months First Line is somewhat scaled down to half strength, operating what is known as 'Winter Line'. The remainder of the First Line moves across to the Second Line to assist with the winter servicing of the team's Hawk aircraft.

In the space of six months, from October to March, the aircraft are given an extensive overhaul that takes between four and sixteen weeks to complete. With the aircraft dismantled, all systems are inspected and tested to ensure that any faults are rectified before the next display season begins.

By the end of January First Line is back to full strength, and all tasks for the coming display season have been allocated. This is a very intensive build-up period, when the new general support crews work up to speed for the following season. This allows time to perfect the operating procedures for the new season.

'The profound sense of ésprit de corps which exists within the Red Arrows' rank and file is unsurpassed in any other RAF unit, and this should come as no surprise. The exhilarating displays and the team's magnetic attraction are seen as a positive and highly successful means of promotion for RAF recruitment.'

Richard J. Caruna

◄

Occasionally the travelling ground crew have to perform a significant task while deploying away from base. Here the pilot's ejector seat is being removed at an event in South Africa.

Throughout the display season the Rectification Ground Crew provide the diagnostic skill and practical expertise to maintain the aircraft between detachments. These technicians cover a variety of trades and have specialised knowledge of propulsion, airframe, electrical, weapons and avionics. In addition there are some technicians from the survival equipment trade.

There are often only a few days between detachments, during which all the aircraft must be restored to pristine condition and prepared for the next deployment. Should an aircraft develop a serious problem while detached, a team of technicians from the rectification crew is quickly despatched to recover it.

Although the Hawk is a reliable, robust aircraft, there are inevitably items that need to be replaced. This responsibility falls to the team's suppliers. The team also has a fleet of fifteen vehicles with its own drivers, who can operate everything from a refuelling bowser to a large articulated tractor and trailer.

Did you know?
The Red Arrows' aircraft are the most intensively serviced in the RAF. Nothing is left to chance, and everything is checked and then double-checked by an extra pair of eyes.

'Today's Red Arrows are the latest in a long line extending over 80 years back into RAF history. Every year hundreds of thousands look up at the sky and marvel at the skills of the pilots. In the best tradition of "showbiz" the Red Arrows combine artistry with danger, yet the standard of excellence necessary to be a team member is far above the normal standards required for even the most dangerous acts.'

Michael Bonello

'Where do the Red Arrows go during the winter?' A surprising number of people are under the impression that the Red Arrows team has little to do in the winter months. Some people even think the team disbands at the end of each display season, but nothing could be further from the truth. In many ways the months from October through to April are busier than the display season itself, as the residents of the villages close to RAF Scampton will readily confirm.

◄
Hawks receive attention from the Rectification Ground Crew in the Red Arrows' hangar during the winter.

The team leader, in conjunction with his pilots, works throughout the winter months choreo-graphing next season's display. The public expects to see some new manoeuvres every year. The engineers, too, are kept busy carrying out extensive servicing on the team's eleven red-painted Hawks so that they should last through the display season with just the minimum of routine maintenance. Every day throughout the season the engineers have to guarantee that at least ten Hawks are service-able and available to fly. To ensure that there are sufficient aircraft to meet the daily flying programme during winter, the team usually borrows two or three Hawks from the Advanced Flying School (No. 4 FTS) at RAF Valley.

◄

An Adour turbofan receives attention from the engine technicians at RAF Scampton.
(Rolls-Royce)

A good formation aerobatic display must be a successful blend of sequences both professional and spectacular. Achieving this requires many hours of intensive training and practice. No matter what difficulties arise, the team must always display to the best possible advantage.

The first steps into the world of tight formation flying are taken by aligning an aircraft with that of the leader. The formating pilot has to concentrate his energies into following the leader's smallest changes quickly, so that his aircraft appears to be an extension of the leader's machine.

To this basic pair other aircraft are gradually added, both on the wing and in line astern, so the formation is slowly built up. Each succeeding outside position requires more concentration to adjust to the exaggerated movements up and down the line. Then the leader begins an aerobatic manoeuvre and appears to fly the team as one.

Throughout he must always fly smoothly and accurately, while positioning his manoeuvres within the confines of the display site. To him it feels like flying a very large and cumbersome aircraft through a fighter tactics

'We would often change between full, rolling and flat shows depending upon weather conditions, and it was pretty rare for displays to be cancelled entirely. Flying in poor conditions was mainly a problem for the leader unless the conditions were very bumpy, when the team members would have a hard time keeping a steady position within a sort of three-foot area.'

Air Cdre 'Dickie' Duckett

Did you know?

The Red Arrows' Hawks are no longer allowed to display lower than 100ft above ground level. This ruling was introduced after a crash off the Brighton sea front on 17 May 1980, when one of the Hawks struck the mast of a yacht.

55

pattern, for, regardless of their place in formation, the pilots must maintain position.

This accurate position-keeping is achieved by each pilot's own considered judgement, and this expertise comes only with constant practice. The leader, too, is displaying his team by 'eyeball' judgement, and will only use his instruments to achieve his desired aerobatic entry and exit speeds, and to maintain his sequence pattern. Even then he usually refers only to his air speed indicator, altimeter and power instruments.

It is essential that each sequence is memorised in full, not only by the leader but by all formating pilots. From the start of the display until its completion some 15 minutes later there are more than twenty formations, manoeuvres and multiple formation changes There are also synchronised items and upwards of thirty smoke 'on' and 'off' calls.

Throughout the selected sequence the team members are in close radio contact with each other, and the leader gives all advisory and executive commands.

Team members acknowledge orders only when they are required to move to change a formation. There is no place for verbosity, and everyone must always be clear, certain, and completely in the picture.

◄◄
Pilots maintain their position in close formation by constantly watching the aircraft ahead of them.
(Jamie Hunter)

'Everyone has their own personality and style but the most important thing is the ability of the individual to work as a team, as well as self-discipline and accuracy. It is important to be able to trust one another when you are up there.'

Flt Lt David Slow, Red 8, 2006

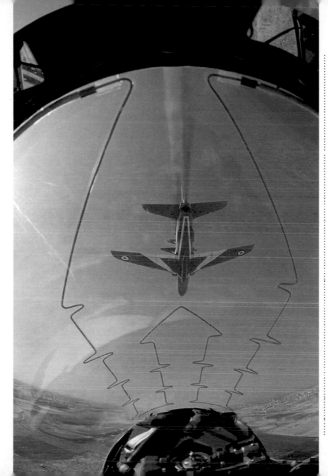

'Some of the Red Arrows' manoeuvres look risky to the spectator at an air display. I know, but few other people realise, how carefully they are planned and how intensively they are practised. I run bigger risks crossing Fleet Street to buy cigars.'

Arthur Gibson, aviation journalist and photographer

◄

A pilot's-eye view as the Hawks fly in line astern, each maintaining its exact position.
(Katsuhiko Tokunaga)

◄ ◄

Eventually the leader begins aerobatic manoeuvres, and appears to fly the team as one.
(Jamie Hunter)

59

➤
Opening its display at Southend-on-Sea, the team flies by in Diamond Nine.

➤➤
Close up of the Diamond Nine – the Reds' signature formation.

61

Reds 1–5 form the front section known as 'Enid', and Reds 6–9 are known as 'Gypo'. Reds 6 and 7 are the 'synchro pair', and perform the stunning manoeuvres during the second half of the display sequence.

Over the years many different display formations have been flown by the team. The one constant, from the time that the Red Arrows was authorised to fly nine aircraft, is the trademark 'Diamond Nine' formation. Other favourite shapes and manoeuvres include Swan, Apollo, Lancaster, Tango, Big Battle, Short Diamond, Eagle, Chevron, Champagne Split, Cyclone, Goose, Heart, Gypo Pass, Vertical Break, Corkscrew, Caterpillar, Mirror Roll, Rollbacks, Gypo Break, Vixen, Viggen, Carousel, Parasol Break, Clover Split and Typhoon. Some of these distinctive Red Arrows' formations are shown on this page and those following.

◀

Swan formation.

◀◀

Viewed from any angle, the Red Arrows 'Diamond' is perfectly formed.
(BAe Military Aircraft)

◄
An 'arrow' piercing a smoke heart.

◄◄
Lancaster bomber-shape formation.

Did you know?
Aircraft types that have flown in formation with the Red Arrows include the Spitfire, Hunter, Vulcan, Concorde, C-130 Hercules and Lockheed U-2, Canadair Tutor, F-117 Nighthawk, Eurofighter Typhoon and Canberra.

➤

Kings Cross.
(Daniel J. March)

Did you know?

If Red 1, the team leader, is unable to fly for any reason, neither can the rest of the team.

◄
Crossover.

Did you know?
On seeing a display, an
elderly lady assumed
that there were no pilots
in the aircraft, and that
they were remotely
controlled from the
ground.

◀
Eagle Bend.

◀◀
Goose cross under.

Rollbacks.

◄
Typhoon fly-past.
(Jamie Hunter)

◄◄
Concorde loop.
(BAe Military Aircraft)

'My tour with the Red Arrows helped me immensely to succeed in civil aviation. The one thing it does for you is to take you out of the RAF. For three years you are not in the RAF at all – you are on stage, you are a performer and you view it that way.'

John Meyers, Red Arrows 1981–3, who now flies
Falcon 20s for FR Aviation

Delta formation.

Synchro Pass and Roll.

Horizontal Synchro Pass.

79

◄
Bomb Burst.

◄◄
Parasol Break.

◄
*Making the most of
coloured smoke.*

◄◄
*Spectacular horizontal
Vixen Break.*

83

➤
*As the team flies over the
Mediterranean the
formation's smoky
shadow is reflected below
one of the Hawks.*
(Action Air Images)

Did you know?

Every performance,
including all practice
and public displays, has
been videoed for
debriefing since 1972.

To refine its skills, the team annually migrates to the Sovereign Base Area of popular RAF station Akrotiri in Cyprus. There it is able to make the most of the fine Mediterranean weather for intensive pre-season training, known as Springhawk. While in Cyprus the team embarks on a typically exhausting schedule, flying three full display practices every day of the working week to fine-tune the manoeuvres.

The whole team works hard to ensure that all of the Hawks are on the line in the morning, ready to make the most of the day's flying. Every member of the team works flat out to ensure that the time spent there is maximised. In the air, the work rate for the pilots is extraordinary. At what seems like just feet above the dark blue of the Mediterranean they fly to the tightest of margins, lining up flap struts and other features on different parts of the aircraft in front to ensure perfect formation alignment. The dark visors of the nine pilots conceal the immense concentration and workload required to stay on the wings of the leader as they paint the sky with red, white and blue smoke, looping, rolling and breaking. 'Good show' comes the call from Red 10 on the ground as they complete the finale 'Vixen Break'.

After each display the pilots immediately go into a detailed debrief, making full use of the excellent video that is filmed from the ground during every performance. This is a vital tool for the pilots, who are typically hard on themselves. Calls of 'short', 'long', 'shallow' or 'deep' from various members of the team indicate how they feel about their positioning within each formation. This detailed debriefing ensures that the team maintains its extraordinary levels of excellence.

Did you know?
The first time the Red Arrows deployed to Cyprus for pre-season training was in the spring of 1980. The usual good weather in April at RAF Akrotiri has been taken advantage of ever since.

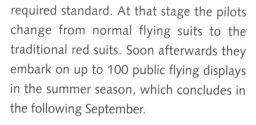
Before displaying in public the team has to obtain a Public Display Authority, the legal permission for it to carry out such displays. This is granted by its Commander-in-Chief at the end of the spring training camp, when he is satisfied the team has reached the required standard. At that stage the pilots change from normal flying suits to the traditional red suits. Soon afterwards they embark on up to 100 public flying displays in the summer season, which concludes in the following September.

➤

Lining up ready to go in the Cyprus spring sunshine during Springhawk training.

*J*amie Hunter describes the never-to-be-forgotten experience of flying with the team during Springhawk at RAF Akrotiri in April 2006.

'OK in the back Jamie?' Flt Lt Damian 'Damo' Ellacott, in his first season with the team, flying Red 3 on the leader's left wing, asks over the intercom as he powers up the Hawk for my first flight this Springhawk with the team. 'Reds check, 2, 3, 4, 5, 6, 7, 8, 9. Akrotiri tower Red Arrows, nine aircraft ready to taxi.' As Sqn Ldr Patounas, 'The Boss', checks us in on the radio, I put a visor down and raise my oxygen mask as Damo checks I am ready to close the canopy.

As we snake in order behind the Boss to Runway 10 at Akrotiri, Damo gives me the safety brief regarding what is planned if we have a problem on take-off. I am happy in the back and the adrenaline is already starting

to flow, and I am just a passenger taking photos. 'Display take-off coming left.' The call from the leader comes as we line up at intervals along the runway. 'Reds rolling . . . now.' Power on, the pilots release the brakes

▼ *Thumbs-up from the back-seat passenger.*

▲ *A trio taking off in close formation.*

and we roll as one. With my feet sitting lightly on the rudder pedals, the inputs come fast from my pilot as he keeps the Hawk arrow-straight on the runway.

Once airborne, the nine Hawks move into tight diamond formation immediately. This is so close, and the positioning is rock-solid formation flying – the pilots are already working incredibly hard. A balance of power, airbrake, rudder and stick are what these highly skilled pilots use to hold this tight position, and it is very impressive from my position as a passenger. Sqn Ldr Patounas calls Red 10 Flt Lt Andy Robins on the ground: 'Nine aircraft ready to display.' We are cleared into a flat practice display over the cliffs at Akrotiri. 'Smoke on . . . go!' The familiar call from Red leader as we begin our first pass over the cliffs practice display line at Akrotiri. 'Coming right . . . now. Holding the bank . . . now. Tightening.' The calls from the front of the formation are constant and they are vital. The team leader's skills guide the team safely around the routine and ensure positioning and timing, and there are so many factors to take into account, not least a strong on-crowd wind today.

◄
Flying to the tightest margins.
(Action Air Images)

For the first half of the flat display it is a sequence of turns in changing formations: Typhoon, Concorde and Short Apollo to name a few. The work rate for the pilots is extraordinary throughout the entire flight. At what seems like just feet above the dark

➤
Rolling above the RAF Akrotiri runway.
(Jamie Hunter)

➤➤
Nine Arrows over the top of a loop.
(Jamie Hunter)

blue of the Mediterranean they are flying to the tightest of margins.

The end of the first half of every display is marked by the team splitting into its two sections, 'Enid' and 'Gypo'. 'Enid' comprises Reds 1–5, and Gypo is formed of Reds 6–9. The second half of the display contains manoeuvres which are much more dynamic, the aim being to keep something happening in front of the crowd at all times. This involves a series of coordinated manoeuvres for the two sections, including Gypo section's famous Synchro crossing manoeuvres, led by Red 6, Synchro leader Flt Lt Si Stevens. For this display I am with Enid, and both sections fly back to the crowdline with highly accurate timing to keep the action in front of the crowd but also to ensure deconfliction between the two sections. We fly the Goose, involving a deep vic formation of our five

Enid Hawks being 'goosed' by Flt Lt Dave Slow in Red 8 flying fast between us. This is followed by twinkle aileron rolls, the rollbacks, and the display culminates with the 7g pull of the Vixen Break. The rollbacks look relatively benign from the ground; in the cockpit the aileron rolls seems incredibly violent, but at the same time they are smooth and controlled and over in a fraction of a second!

After 30 minutes we are running in for the break over the runway. One last g-saturated pull and we are downwind for landing in sequence. A quick check from Damo that my toes are clear of the brakes, and we turn finals and grease down on the Akrotiri runway. The sweat is pouring off me, so goodness knows how the pilots have remained so cool. As we taxi in I am cleared to replace my ejector seat and canopy safety pins, and as we come to a halt we are met

95

➤

Pilots are working hard to maintain the tight formation through the manoeuvres.

(Jamie Hunter)

by the dedicated ground crews. As the canopy opens, the engines have spooled down and Damo is already climbing out. 'See you inside,' he says. Now the engineers swing into action to prepare the jets for the next practice.

The team pilots immediately go into a detailed debrief, making full use of the excellent video. Sitting in the brief, I struggle to see the errors, but these pilots are talking literally in inches of positioning, hence the extraordinary levels of excellence maintained by the Red Arrows.

➤

Airbrakes out to slow the Hawks' speed during a tricky manoeuvre.
(Action Air Images)

➤➤

7g is pulled in the Vixen Break.

➤
Gnats were first painted in Yellowjacks colours at No. 4 FTS in 1964.
(Glen Moreman)

APPENDIX I – SPECIFICATIONS

FOLLAND (HAWKER SIDDELEY) GNAT T.1

Engine: One Bristol Siddeley Orpheus
Mk 100/101 turbojet of 4,230lb static thrust

Wingspan: 24ft 0in (7.32m)

Wing area: 150sq ft (16.26sq m)

Length: 31ft 9in (9.68m)

Overall height: 9ft 7in (2.93m)

Maximum speed: Mach 0.95; 640mph
(625 kt/1,030km/h)/Mach 1.15 in a shallow
dive

Maximum weight: 8,914lb (4,043kg)

Accommodation: Two, in tandem

In November 1953 Bristol had begun to develop
the Orpheus turbojet because NATO liked the
idea of light fighter and ground-attack aircraft.
The engine proved a godsend for the Gnat,
which first flew on 18 July 1955.

In August 1955 the Ministry of Supply placed
an order for six Gnat fighters for development

flying, but the type was not adopted by the RAF.
However, by the latter half of 1957 the Gnat's
potential as a two-seat trainer was realised, and
an initial pre-production order was placed for
fourteen aircraft. In February 1960 this was
followed by an initial production order for thirty
Gnat T.1s.

The first Gnat T.1 flew on 31 August 1959,
and the type first entered service with the RAF at
the CFS, Little Rissington, in February 1962. It
replaced the Vampire T.11 as the RAF's standard
advanced trainer in Flying Training Command.

The first Gnat course at No. 4 FTS began in
early 1963. In the following year the school
formed its own aerobatic team with yellow-
painted Gnats, known as the Yellowjacks. In
1965 it became the Red Arrows.

Gnats remained in service as the RAF's
standard advanced trainer until replaced by the
Hawk at RAF Valley in November 1978. The

Gnats were flown by the CFS/4 FTS (centre), the Yellowjacks (right) and the Red Arrows (left).

Did you know?

The Gnat had very light and sensitive controls, so it was easy to over-control, particularly in pitch when the 'g' came on coming out of a loop.

Red Arrows Gnats gave their last display at Valley on 16 September 1979.

Gnats with the Reds

A total of twenty-eight Gnats flew with the Red Arrows during the type's 14 years with the team. Though some aircraft were withdrawn from use while attached to the team, they were not necessarily struck off RAF charge. Several Gnats from No. 4 FTS, Valley, were attached to the Red Arrows early in 1968, while other team aircraft were cleared following the temporary grounding of the type, and these are not included in the following list:
XP501, XP505, XP514, XP515, XP531, XP533, XP535, XP538, XP539, XP541, XR537, XR540, XR545, XR571, XR572, XR574, XR955, XR977, XR981, XR986, XR987, XR991, XR992, XR993, XR994, XR995, XR996, XS101, XS107 and XS111.

HAWKER SIDDELEY (BAe) HAWK T.1/T.1A

Engine: One Rolls-Royce/Turboméca Adour Mk 151 turbofan of 5,200lb static thrust
Wingspan: 30ft 9.75in (9.39m)
Wing area: 180sq ft (16.72sq m)
Length: 39ft 2in (11.96m)
Overall height: 13ft 1in (3.98m)
Maximum speed: 622mph (1,000km/h) at sea level
Maximum weight: 16,260lb (7,374kg)
Accommodation: Two, in tandem

The Hawk first flew in 1974, and entered RAF service on 4 November 1976, both as an advanced trainer and as a tactical weapons training aircraft. It was designed to replace the Gnat and Hunter T.7, as well as performing some of the roles of the Jet Provost, in a major rationalisation of RAF training programmes from 1977 onwards. A strong and rugged trainer, it

Did you know?
The team has appeared in many TV programmes, including: *Surprise, Surprise; This is Your Life; Jim'll Fix it* and *How do they do that?*

has been designed to cut operating and maintenance costs, and has a long fatigue life. It was the first British aircraft to be designed from the outset using metric measurement.

A total of 175 Hawks entered service with the RAF. Flight tests demonstrated that the Hawk exceeded all of its performance requirements and, although supersonic speed was not

➤

A Red Arrows Hawk armed with an Aden cannon and Sidewinder air-to-air missiles.
(BAe Military Aircraft)

➤➤

The Reds maintain their precise formation as they taxi in after a display.

specified, the prototype, XX154, exceeded Mach 1.04 in a shallow dive in February 1975.

The Red Arrows received eleven Hawks between August and November 1979 from the production aircraft for the RAF. They were fitted with the smoke system and given the distinctive red, white and blue colour scheme. In other respects the Hawks flown by the team are in the same configuration as the rest of the fleet, and have been similarly modified and upgraded in the intervening years. Through the period of the Cold War the team's Hawks could be armed with 30mm cannon and Sidewinder air-to-air missiles and used to augment the UK's air defence forces. More than three decades after the Hawk prototype's first flight a much-developed version remains in production with BAE Systems and has been ordered by the RAF.

Red Arrows Hawks

Up to the end of 2005 some twenty-three different Hawks had been flown by the Red Arrows during the summer seasons since 1979. They are:

XX179, XX227, XX233, XX237, XX241, XX243, XX250, XX251, XX252, XX253, XX257, XX259, XX260, XX262, XX264, XX266, XX292, XX294, XX297, XX304, XX306, XX307 and XX308.

Did you know?

In still air a BAe Hawk with total engine failure can only glide, at best, 2 miles for every 1,000ft of height.

APPENDIX II – MILESTONES

1965 **1 February:** Delivery to the CFS of the Red Arrows' first Gnat T.1, XR540. This had also been the Yellowjacks' first aircraft.

1965 **May:** Formation of Red Arrows at RAF Fairford.

1965 **6 May:** The Red Arrows' first public appearance at Clermont-Ferrand during the French Air Force Meeting de l'Air.

1965 **14 May:** The Reds received the last production Gnat T.1, XS111, to bring the team's strength to nine aircraft (of which seven were used for displays, together with an airborne spare).

1965 **15 May:** First UK public appearance of the Red Arrows, at the Biggin Hill Air Fair.

1965 At the end of the 1965 season the Royal Aero Club awarded the Red Arrows its Britannia Trophy 'for the British aviator or aviators accomplishing the most meritorious performance in aviation during the year'.

1966 Sqn Ldr Ray Hanna became leader of the Red Arrows and performed eighty-five displays with them that year, including SBAC Show at Farnborough.

1966 The team made a tour of the Mediterranean, including Cyprus, Malta and Jordan.

1966 **8 July:** First display with nine pilots.

1966 **6 August:** First nine-ship display in the UK, at Brawdy.

1967 The beginning of the 1967 season was delayed following grounding of the RAF Gnats after structural weakness was discovered in the tail units of some aircraft.

1967 For this season the entire fin was painted with red, white and blue flashes, with a Union flag superimposed on the white segment.

1967	Red Arrows reduced to seven aircraft.
1968	50th Anniversary of the RAF. Red Arrows flew over a hundred shows during the year.
1968	The team was permanently increased in size to nine, and the new Diamond Nine Gnats formation became the team's symbol.
1969	Pilots' names were painted in white lettering beneath the canopies of the aircraft.
1969	Previously a detachment of the CFS, the Red Arrows was established permanently as a standard RAF squadron.
1969	**12 December:** The team's first aircraft loss. During practice, one aircraft caught fire. Another team member radioed its pilot, who ejected, along with the pilot of another Gnat in the formation who 'banged out' in error.
1971	**20 January:** In a tragic accident at RAF Kemble two aircraft were lost and four pilots killed. This was the team's first fatal accident.
1972	**17 May:** The team embarked on its first US tour for Operation Longbow.
1973	**13 June:** An authenticated crowd of 650,000 people watched the Red Arrows' display at Lisbon, Portugal, a figure not exceeded until Sydney, Australia, in 1996.
1974	Start of the display season postponed due to the worldwide energy crisis.
1975	The fuel crisis continued, and only fifty-six displays were flown in the year.
1977	**26 June:** The 1,000th display by Gnats was performed at the International Air Tattoo at RAF Greenham Common.
1978	The white nose flash was 'broken' to accommodate the words 'Royal Air Force' in white lettering.

1979	The first pre-season training camp was held at RAF Akrotiri, Cyprus.
1979	**August:** The first BAe Hawk was delivered to the Red Arrows. The ninth was handed over on 15 November.
1979	**September:** Final Gnat public displays, at the Battle of Britain Days at RAF Abingdon and St Athan.
1979	By the end of the team's 15th successive season its Gnats had flown 1,292 displays.
1979	**Winter:** Conversion to the BAe Hawk.
1979	**15 November:** The team carried out its first display with nine Hawk T.1s, over the BAE factory airfield at Bitteswell, Leicestershire.
1980	**13 March:** First public appearance with the Hawk was a display at Episkopi, Cyprus.
1980	**April:** Official permission was granted for the team to have its own badge and the motto 'Eclat'.
1980	**6 April:** First UK public display using the Hawks, at Sywell, Northants.
1980	**17 May:** Hawk XX262 was written off when it hit a yacht mast during a display off the coast at Brighton. The pilot ejected safely. The was the first Reds aircraft to crash in public.
1981	The Red Arrows Charitable Trust was established, endorsed subsequently by a policy statement from the Ministry of Defence.
1981	A special display was flown over Caernarfon Castle for the wedding of the Prince of Wales.
1983	**10 March:** The team officially moved from RAF Kemble, its home since 1966, to RAF Scampton, where it arrived on 5 April, on return from Cyprus.
1983	**3 May:** The team departed on its second North American tour, the first since it re-equipped with the Hawk.

1984	**21 March:** Hawk XX251 crashed at Akrotiri during spring training.
1984	**31 August:** Hawk XX257 ditched in the sea off Sidmouth, Devon, due to engine compressor failure.
1986	**12 June:** The RAF Aerobatic Team embarked on a 17-day Far East Tour named Eastern Hawk, giving 22 displays in 15 countries.
1986	The Red Arrows' 2,000th display, given at Bournemouth/Hurn.
1989	The 25th anniversary of the Red Arrows was celebrated with a display at RAF Scampton involving six aerobatic teams.
1990	The Red Arrows visited the Soviet Union for the first time. On its way back the team gave a display in Budapest, Hungary.
1990	**15 September:** The largest fly-past in which the team has ever participated: the 168-aircraft Battle of Britain 50th anniversary fly-past over Buckingham Palace and RAF Abingdon.
1991	**26 August:** The team formated for the first time with the RAF's Vulcan B.2 bomber XH558 at the Great Warbirds Air Display at West Malling.
1991	**18–23 September:** The Reds hosted the Sukhoi Su-27s of the Soviet Air Force Russian Knights team at RAF Scampton for the duration of the latter's first international appearance, which included displays at Leuchars and Finningley.
1992	**September:** To mark the retirement of the RAF's last Avro Vulcan, the Red Arrows flew in formation with XH558 at Cranfield.
1992	**September:** A unique formation was flown at Bratislava, Slovakia, with a Red Arrows Hawk joining a White Albatros Aero L-39, a

◀◀

Marking the retirement of the last Vulcan, the Arrows flew with the V-bomber at the Cranfield Airshow in September 1992.

Patrouille de France Alpha Jet, Frecce Tricolori MB.339, Patrulla Aguila Aviojet and Russian Test Pilots' Sukhoi Su-27.

1993 **19 September:** Start of the Reds' third North American tour. Fourteen displays were flown in the USA, plus one in Canada.

1995 The team gave 136 displays, the highest number flown in any one calendar year.

1995 **23 August:** The Red Arrows' 3,000th display was given at the official opening of the Dartmouth Royal Regatta.

1995 **October to February 1996:** The team embarked on a world tour including the Middle East, South Africa, Asia (and LIMA 95 in Malaysia) and Australia.

1996 **26 January:** It is estimated that the Reds' display was watched by the largest ever number of spectators at Sydney on Australia Day – nearly a million people.

1996 **21 February:** On its return to the UK after four months away, the team landed back at RAF Cranwell, its new home following the closure of Scampton.

1997 As part of BAE's export sales drive the Red Arrows displayed at the Dubai Air Show.

2000 **21 December:** The Reds returned to RAF Scampton following a review of basing requirements.

2002 **4 June:** The Red Arrows took part in a formation with a British Airways Concorde over London to mark Her Majesty The Queen's Golden Jubilee.

2002 **August–September:** The team made a short visit to Canada.

2003 **25 September:** Exercise Eastern Hawk 03 began, and the team undertook a five-week goodwill tour

◄◄

RAF exchange pilot Sqn Ldr Richie Matthews flying a USAF F-117A Nighthawk 'stealth' fighter with the Red Arrows at the Royal International Air Tattoo in July 2003.

to the Middle and Far East. The tour was supported by industry, including BAE Systems and Rolls-Royce.

2003 **17 December:** The centenary of powered flight was marked by the Reds with a fly-past over the opening of the RAF Museum Hendon's new 'Milestones of Flight' building.

2006 **March:** The team practised for two weeks at Tanagra at the invitation of the Hellenic Air Force, before flying to Cyprus for Springhawk.

2006 **May:** A tour to the Middle East, India and southern Europe delayed the start of the team's UK season until 10 June.

➤
The team leader and fellow pilots prepare to leave their aircraft at the end of a busy day.